T0064263

Scattered Shades
of Henna

Scattered Shades of Henna

Mojib Nashtar

Translated by
Prof A K Nagar

PARTRIDGE
A Penguin Random House Company

To order additional copies of this book, contact
Partridge India
000 800 10062 62
orders.india@partridgepublishing.com

www.partridgepublishing.com/india

Contents

The Creator... 4

Paradise Lost 5

Ghalib's Poetry... 6

A Night At A Nursing Home 7

From Dusk to Dawn 8

Stages of Life.. 9

Night 10

Even Petals Feel Shy 11

Grief Laden heart 12

Cipher.. 13

Protest..14

An Interval..15

Restlessness 16

On the Canvas of Water..17

Garden..18

Transformation 19

Tribal Dance.. 20

Corruption...21

Wolves 22

Conflict 23

Serpents' Descendants.. 24

Time 25

Representative 26

Whisper 27

Shame 28

Shame … 29

Cellphone... 30

Frightened Cloud 31

Old Age Home.. 32

Silence.. 33

The Majestic Court.. 34

Fire of Dowry..35

Dejection 36

Effort 37

My Village, My Home 38

Invocation 39

Inroduction.. 40

Mirrors.. 41

New Year 42

Kalpana Chawla.. 43

Gift - 1.. 44

Gift - 2..45

Grave Moments.. 46

Rainy Season.. 47

The Earthly Heaven 48

Yashodhara... 49

Eerie Silence.. 50

Longing 51

Queen of Beauty 52

Camps of the Aged.. 53

Life's Footpath 54

Marching Steps of a Village...55

About the Author and Translator

Mojib Nashtar is an accomplished Urdu poet. His poetic journey spans over five decades. He has published four books including *Satrah Qatre* (a collection of Haikus) and *Hindustani Tarailey* (a collection of Triolet – a French form of poetry). His poetry is a fine blend of classical trend and modern current. His language style is unique in the sense that some of his poems are in chaste Urdu, some in pure Hindi and some in Hindustani and all this with much ease and spontaneity.

Prof A K Nagar is a former college teacher and acting Principal of a Teacher's Training college. He has taught methodology of teaching English to trainee teachers for about three and a half decades. He has keen interest in Hindi and English literature. His entry into Urdu poetry through Hindi transcription makes his translation work a unique one in which Hindi, Hindustani and Urdu languages are made easily comprehensible to readers.

Preface

Scattered Shades of Henna, reflecting the changing style of Urdu poetry, is my fifth poetic collection. The readers will find four different types of poems in it which, I am sure, will reflect the change in the style of Urdu poetry.

Modern research has established that Quli Qutb Shah (1565-1611) is the first poet of Urdu poetry. He was the fifth ruler of Qutb Shahi dynasty of Golkunda in South India. He wrote hundreds of poems and all these poems are the examples of rhymed verses. This pattern of writing rhymed verses continued onward, in all its brightness and splendor, up to the time of Doctor Iqbal and Josh Malihabadi and even today.

With the beginning of the second decade of the twentieth century, there came a revolutionary change in almost all the departments of human life, and in consonance with that, a change in Urdu poetry across the world was adequately visible. The western style of literature too had its impact on Urdu poetry which resulted in the birth of, besides the rhymed verses, three more different types of poetry from 1920 till this date. Now there are four formats of Urdu poetry.

The readers will enjoy all these four formats of writing poetry in my present collection - Scattered *Shades of Henna.* This collection consists of 15 rhymed verses, one each blank verse and prose poetry and 34 free verses. All these 51 Urdu poems are beautifully translated in English by Prof. A. K.

Nagar during his stay in USA. I find no words to express my heart-felt gratitude to him for his excellent work. It seems my work has been recreated by him.

Now that this book is in the hands of my critic readers, I have nothing to say about it. It's for them to evaluate my work.

Mojib Nashtar
Delhi
12th day of July, 2015

Dedicated to
my esteemed readers

The Creator

He is the Creator,
He is eternal.
His gift - the Universe--
The moon, the stars, the galaxies,
The earth, the sky,
Moon and the Jupiter,
The wisdom of prophets,
The gravitational pull
Between static and revolving planets.
Biting chill of winter,
Scorching heat of summer,
Existence of genii and humans,
Appearance of fire and dust,
Fascinating sight of twilight and horizon,
Dying breath of setting sun,
Shuffling of morn and eve.
Forests, mountains, earth and oceans,
Those countless miracles of nature
And the blessing of all-pervasive God.
He is the Creator,
He is eternal,
His gift - the Universe

Paradise Lost

Sun, Moon and the galaxy,
All the inhabitants of the paradise,
Confident are they in their attire,
Aware of nakedness rare in their nature.

Till yesterday, we too were stationed in the garden of heaven,
Like sweet odour on the bed of flowers.

Satan came, tempted and led us,
Alas! From heaven to earth, did we fall
To bear the burden of tears and tribulations.

Now that our heart waits for the doomsday
But maybe we see the garden of paradise some day.

Ghalib's Poetry

Moon, stars, galaxies,
And floating clouds
On the sky;
Bright shining face of the world,
Troubled dark locks of night.
A world
Dancing to a new tune,
Reflected in every poem.
Face- to- face
With life's intoxicating goblets -
Such is Ghalib's poetry.

A Night At A Nursing Home

Why is the night so long?
Dry tears in someone's eyes;
Sad are some faces;
Still life bound by rules?
I know I am ill,
Yet I am awake.
I am amazed
And wonder -
If I am sick,
Why is this cell sick too?
Look at that bottle on the stand,
That soft bottle with colourless fluid,
So miser to ooze out,
Drop by drop,
And then swallowed by the aching veins.
Ill-omen is cast on the ceiling of the cell,
Weeping and crying,
Madness everywhere - on the walls
And on the doors,
Wailing and crying, but why?
I have life in me,
Strength in me,
I am alive, indeed.

From Dusk to Dawn

The Sun's boat amidst the ocean
Sank and vanished.
Appeared then the eve;
Appeared and passed stealthily.
Next, the night's extended tresses,
Helping to raise the nocturnal business of bubbling night.
Tattered everwhere the light's lappet,
And the life dancing in its tavern.
Be it so; very soon from the Sun's persona
The light will spring.

Stages of Life

Childhood:
Sweet lullaby
Everywhere in courtyard

Youth:
Dazzling bright,
Making the Sun blush

Old Age:
Unsteady steps,
Tossed from door to door

Night

Morn's rhythm,
Eve's note,
Night remiss,
Sky's tumultuous stars and moon,
Joy and mirth of cup and goblet,
Moments of fun and merriment,
Fragrance of buds and flowers,
Yes, and the whole sky,
Pride of dark and muddled sight.
Leaving all this scene behind,
My sweetheart Night departed.

Even Petals Feel Shy

So thin, soft and tender are her lips,
That make even flower petals feel shy.

Deep intoxicating eyes,
Searching for life.

In the glaze of her face,
The whole world is glowing.

Grief Laden heart

Not a single drop of tears
In dried up tearless eyes
Yet weeping, running tears,
Like empty heart at times brimming
With countless unexpressed emotions
In midst of dark nights,
Of childlike thoughts,
Tired as I am,
Still keeping the burden
Of my laden heart and searching eyes.

Cipher

Cipher is a number,
Nay, it's more than that.
Cipher is a beginning,
Cipher is an end.
Cipher is a number,
Nay, it's more than that.....

On a beautiful moon-like forehead,
It's a sparkling dot.
Cipher is our globe,
Cipher is a pendant on hair-parting.
Every drop a pearl,
Every particle a diamond.
Tear hanging from her eye-lid
Is a cipher too.
Nuclear era,
Distance and time
All unsteady.
Man muzzy,
Ever contracting distance
Eventually cipher.
Cipher is a number,
Nay, it's more than that......

May this happen -
The whole universe
Rumpled suddenly,
Cleaving cipher by itself.
Cipher is a number,
Nay, it's more than that.

Protest

From the womb of Tunisia
Arose a spark of fire,
That englulfed the entire Middle East.
Protest, fiery protests everywhere.
On the supreme land of Egypt,
Spread the protests instantly.
Know not how many countries were engulfed -
Algeria, Yemen, Jordan and Oman
Stream of blood flowed through Libya,
That saw the downfall of Moammar Gaddafi,
And the dismissal of Hosni Mubarak,
Only to get a shelter in Sharm-el-Sheikh.
Remember the human life is short lived,
The crown and the throne for a few days,
And then the people's protest all supreme.

An Interval

Spotless white
As milky flakes,
Oh! silvery bright,
Tight close to the mother's breasts: 'Chaandni'
Perhaps -
I have seen her,
May be twenty two years ago!

As bright as
The Moon,
Yea, silvery bright,
A little girl,
An innocent kid.
In her lap like 'Chaandni'.
Years rolled by, but the face is the same,
As if a flower embracing another flower

Restlessness

No more resonates
The flute of peace
In my village.

Under the shelter of glass,
And in the shade, the Sun scorches.

It's the season of blossoming flowers,
But I have brought thorns to my feet,
From the splendid garden.

Come, let's go
Across the Ganges,
Come, sit in my tiny boat.

On the Canvas of Water

'Majnu' used to write 'Laila' here and there on sands,
But Laila still a pious legacy of Majnu.
On the canvas of water are written
Names of many jovial Lailas,
Beautiful, delicate Lailas.
But are now scattered all over -
In Hollywood,
In Bollywood,
In China,
In Japan,
In Egypt and Turkey,
In India and Pakistan.
More than twenty alive,
All famous,
Once happy,
Now weak and feeble,
No radiance on their face,
Ah! no attraction

Garden

A small garden that I have,
Me the gardener,
And my wife the tenderer,
A flower....
Heart charming Rose from the flower's family,
Beautiful and full of modesty....
Intoxicating climate of our garden that it has,
Soft, cool wind blowing around...
Blessings from the pious people,
Grace of Almighty,
And then the arrival of tender buds,
And the approaching of Spring,
All-encompassing attraction from every direction,
Freshness on every branch, every flower and every pathway.
Newly grown tender petals, new saplings all over,
Colour and fragrance of the garden at its zenith.

Transformation

Revolution, always ready to strike,
Movement of azure sky,
Existence of living and non-living,
The order of this existence changes of its own.
Even graceful gait of enchanting universe is temporary,
Fragrance of flowers got distracted in dream,
Candle flame at bed chamber burnt out before day-break,
Lifeless portraits of transitory world seem restless.
Yes, the Solitude is the companion,
Shadows of some sweet dreams,
Graceful gait of some ebony body.
Revolution is perpetual,
Life only a dream.

Tribal Dance

Amidst rocky hills, a tumultous evening crowd,
In the lap of small dwellings,
An ecstatic dance in progress.
Lovely women in one row,
Robust men in another,
Deeply engaged to the dancing tunes,
Anklets are the clanking shackles,
Red turbans on their heads,
Though scantily dressed.
Deadly drunk drinking rice wine,
Unmindful of the surroundings,
Women too sunk and inebriated,
But colourfully dressed,
Akin to troops in array on a dancing floor,
Drums calling the fun players,
Arousing body movement,
Dancing steps in an amazing evening,
Men and women to and fro,
One by one, with the cry of drum,
Spell bound by the magic,
Entire jungle woke up listening melodious noise,
Songs in a wedding procession,
Boats of throbbing hearts on a dance floor,
Sailing like gondolas,
Entire surroundings enchanted by deep ecstasy
Life soaked in merrymaking the whole night,
O friends! Look, the captivating scene sailed us through
To the sweet morning in a cosy basket.

Corruption

Alas! The Sun bereft of light,
Tyrant Sea sucking countless rivers,
The Coast a silent spectator.

Trees and plants - target of tyranny,
With cruel winds roaring day and night,
Deafening hue and cry all over.

Proud Lion on a regal throne,
Mice sad, fearing cats,
Who will bell the cats?
Silence everywhere, you and me too.

At last,
Time yawns, inclement weather changes,
Voice of protest reverberates all over,
End bribery! End corruption!
The whole society rising to a new culture.

Wolves

Was she a Hindu or a Christian or a Muslim or a Sikh?
I only know this much -
Extremely beautiful was she,
A bright shining morning star.
She hid Kaba in her veil,
Temple close abreast.
Beauty and radiance of church on her forehead,
Grandeur of Gurudwara in her eyes.
Embodiment of purity and chastity,
A poet's fancy, the fairest of womenfolk,
Whoever she was, she was the noblest of all,
Alas! She was killed, the Envy of Freshness wiped out.
A morning of wailing from the heavens,
Still the wolves unashamed,
Those wicked incapable beasts!

Conflict

Even while close to you,
It's difficult to live.
That every particle of the fascinating city
Seems to be my deadly foe.
So many taboos,
And noise for prohibitions.
If I go far far away from you,
Even then, it's difficult to live,
'Cause it's you people's life,
That gives radiance to my life,
And kindles my soul.

Serpents' Descendants

Trees of old relations,
Of great relations,
Have now grown old.
Serpents now inhabit
The sleeves of old, pious relations.

This mystery still persists
But all these birds know,
Those who perch on the branches
Those who tell with their twitter ---
No one knows how many people these snakes have bitten.
Trees of old relations
Are on the brink,
They blossom in the Spring,
They wait for the great storm,
But these descendants of serpents
Are still on top.

Time

With light comes dawn,
And there appears the King of the East.
The world awakened from dream,
Garden in full blossom with flowers and creepers.

Trees laden with flowers,
Birds up in the sky, with wings apart.
Welcome Noon,
Charm and beauty of the youthful Sun,
All indulging in the business of life,
Short is the life's noon time as well,
Prime of life - friend of fleeting moments.
It vanishes with a blink of an eye.
And then comes the evening for a few rapid moments.
Night! thou has your own arrangements,
Moon, stars, galaxies,
The charm of bride,
The reign of darkness;
Every pleasure house is awake,
Playing game of cup and bottle of pure wine,
Dream with eyes open;
Oh Ecstasy! come back to senses,
And respect Time.

Representative

Whoever may be our representative,
O people, mark, that's our boon.
No one in this world is pure and pious.
Yes, for a very long time, we and you
Churned the Sea,
But till today,
Every shell found
Empty of precious pearl.

Nature's hand
Spread countless stars on the sky;
But --
All around is that dim light,
And that too in a fluster.
Thus, behind the curtain,
The Universe spreads its magic.

Whisper

Nay, sensational verse is no balm to aching heart;
Under the shadow of silence treads the fascinating thought.
Moon's beam moving gracefully on the flowery bed,
Scratching sound producing unpleasant noise.
Silence: swaggering wave, dancing goblet,
Sweetheart's affinity, state of solitude, joy and mirth,
Body touch, whisper, familiar words, paradise to blessed ears.

Shame

'Tun, tun, tun, tun'
Bird of Time flying high,
Wings apart,
Up in the sky,
Like rockets
Bursting loudly.
Bird of Time flying high.
'Tun,..............'
First period -
Period of mathematics,
Mr. Verma,
Slim and lanky,
A college master,
Writing on the black-board--
Alpha beta gamma theta,
And then those algebraic riddles,
Followed by geometrical puzzles,
And lo! there goes everything with one duster sweep,
But watch carefully,
Watch those dancing
Fair faces
On the dark board.
Rouge on the cheek of 'Neelu',
Fresh as cheese,
'Azra's' rosy lips,
Rosy as cups of tea.
Bird of Time flying high,
Wasted two years for nothing.

Shame ...

I am the BDO's PEON,
BDO Sahib's wife, I know
Is a woman like 'Neelu' -
Rouge of 'Neelu's' cheeks,
As fresh as cheese,

A small car parked there
That's the car of SDO Saheb
'Zaidi' is the Saheb,
Thin and slim,
Small stature.
In that car,
A beautiful blossoming face,
I know, I know that face,
That's SDO Saheb's wife,
Saheb's Begum, I know,
Is a woman like 'Azra'.

'Azra's' rosy lips,
Like cup of rosy tea,
'Azra's' gleaming face,
Nay, I feel ashamed to look at.

Cellphone

Needle-thread-carved words paralyzed,
No season now sings any ballad,
Nor the lovelorn melancholy song.

Today windows don't converse one to one,
Flower petals
Not seen perched
On the pages of books.
Though so near yet so distant,
But never to be perturbed by his memories.
Even the moonlit night gives no pain,
Even night may be dark,
Clouds may sail in the sky,
But I am carefree - ignorant of all.
He may live anywhere,
But he is my co-traveller,
He is all – the sun, the moon,
I am only his light,
And now between us both is -
A Cellphone.

Frightened Cloud

Hard to speak, these days, the miserable condition of clouds,
Restless as they are day and night.
For days they remained suspended from the sky roof,
Only to fall on highlands and mountains.

One day, the Earth mumbled to them on cellphone -
'Dear Brother! tell me the cause of your annoyance.'

Thus answered the leader of the clouds, at last -
'Dear Sister! difficult to explain,
As it's not good to open the secret of heart.'

You have become a slaughter house these days,
Confusion, commotion and panic everywhere,
Bloodshed, plundering - all at its zenith.
Everybody naked in the same bathing pool -
Thieves, dacoits and watchmen together.
Difficult to live in the country,
Impossible in cities,
Moral degradation all over.

Old Age Home

These days, old age home
Is my rest house,
And a small car for sight-seeing and recreation.

Pleasant was my childhood:
Kisses and caresses of parents,
Absolute carefree life,
Charm and attraction all the way.

Slowly descended the youth:
Spring of life, mirthful day and night,
Flourishing business,
A jewellery shop,
A bungalow and two apartments,
Gate and the gatekeeper,

Four sons and daughters.
But what a pity! they all
Lost their mother's love.

Both my daughters, their husbands
Settled in Germany.
Both my sons in Africa.
Today, I am all alone in my own city,
Ground under constant coercion of cycle of time,
Losing nervous control of hand and feet,
No enjoyment of life even in dreams,
Handing over my entire business
To my brother-in-law's son.
These days, old age home
Is my rest house,
Waiting for eternal sleep.

Silence

Hilarious music no solace to my aching heart;
Silence is needed.
I look at the undercurrents in the deep,
Wandering clouds in the sky,
Light silvery moonlight,
Petals looking like lips,
Fading line of ripple's smile,
A new born moon on sky's duvet.
Animated dance in the backdrop of silence,
Silvery voice, familiar talk,
Sweetheart's proximity, warmth of her body,
And all that gay and mirth.

The Majestic Court

Countless are the pages of the world,
Some giving light, some relinquishing,
Some are ugly and some very dim.
Moon is proud of its borrowed light,
Every celestial body looks like a beautiful galaxy.
Universe and the meta-universe --
Whose majestic court are they?
To reach His court,
How easy and difficult is the path?
On the shelf is lying
The hermit's book,
The mirror is the drunkard's goblet,
Everyone has his own glass and his own goblet,
But restless is the broken heart.

Fire of Dowry

Her hip movement
Had celestial attraction.
Moon and stars ready to sacrifice
For her bright forehead.
More charming was she
Than the Venus idol.
What happened to
The honour of life's tavern?
Sparkling bright eyes.
Rich in deeds,
Rich in voice,
Rich in manner she was.
A graceful gait of Spring breeze!
Full bright Moon,
Prosperity of craving desert,
A countryside damsel.
Countenance -
A perfect blend of beauty and coyness.
Rich in every aspect.
Alas! Her parents were poor.
Lovely, tender and delicate as she was,
But for mannerism
Was she a perfect model of life.
But we now hear -
She is no more,
Burnt into the fire
Of DOWRY.

Dejection

In your absence,
When I put my feet
On the threshold of your village,
Fast ran my heartbeat,
And I found no ground underneath ----
Before my eyes was the advent of twilight
And crimson red firmament.

But --
The old banyan tree looked at me with great expectations,
But afraid of darkness,
I did not stop ----

I reached your home,
Stealthily I walked upto the doorstep,
Fast ran my heartbeat,
And I found no ground underneath ----

Stopped for a while,
And then
Knocked at the door -----

The servant of your grandpa
Appeared fast,
The servant said to me:
You all have gone to Shimla,
But will be back soon ------

Effort

In the garden, countless flowers blossom,
But what! Even if it's a season of blossom,
I apprehend some unforeseen to happen -
Flowers may fade before they fully blossom,
Death will continue to stalk.
But stop not, a satellite phone
May send a message to the discerning -
Continue your efforts to discover,
Those sitting idle
May repent the whole life.

My Village, My Home

Despite owning a home,
For full twenty two odd years'
I kept moving
From door to door
Like skies
Yet full sixty years of my life,
I spent splendidly
Completely devoted to my job.
Now I have come back to my village,
On a pension.

Now I have my village,
My children,
And a beautiful home in my village.
A huge yard strewn with flowers,
Greenery all around,
And yes, a well and a *lath-kundi#* too.

Lovely colourful morning,
Winds touching and kissing trees and plants,
Birds chirping.
Ah! We are in our village at last,
Everything so comforting,
Heart brewing with confidence.

#lath-kundi -- In some rural parts of India, water is drawn from wells with the help of a big bamboo, on one side of it is tied a heavy stone and on other side a bucket is hung with a rope. The weight of the stone helps to draw up the bucket filled with water which is emptied and again put back in the well.

Invocation

Bless the plants of thoughts with fruits of words,
And make their branches pregnant with meaning.

My boat of craftmanship is in delusion,
Sail it with the waves of reality.

To the colourless buds of garden's sagacity,
Give the freshness of morn and the colour of fresh rose.

In the course of transmission, spread the fragrance of fresh rose,
And fill the robes of thoughts with that fragrance.

I pray - let the stagnant blood flow and faded buds bloom,
Give the message of sunrise to the gloomy dark nights.

No prejudice towards masters of politics,
But I pray give right direction to the aspirants.

Make my vision to sublimity equal to Pleiadas,
Give vision's beauty to my earthy body.

I admit that the tree has grown big,
Prune the worn out thoughts, I pray.

In the world's showcase, I am perplexed and amazed,
O, my Lord! give a glow of vision to my eye.

My cup of art is empty,
O, the Cup-bearer! fill it with blessings.

Inroduction

Why ye need to know me now?
I am the tears rolling down thy cheeks.

What is this sweet smell from the veil of my thoughts?
Know ye, it is the fragrance spreading from thy scattered locks.

Methink thou art an envious doe,
And me the stag wandering in the deep forest,

Even if I go far, far into the distance,
Ye need to know me every bit,

At times I'm 'Nashtar', at times I'm soothing balm, may be
a physician,
If you think it's magic, be it so.

Mirrors

Fixed, even today, in the picture gallery of my heart,
O, my friend! Know not how many mirrors of memories.
Some reflecting the heart ravishing sights of my childhood,
And some the prime of my youthful days.

Still some manifesting the beauty of autumn,
Some bringing the colours of spring,
Some distressed love and painful solitude,
Some showing jovial and jolly pictures.

Look those rosy cheeks with crimson flower work,
Grey eyes with dark lining,
Sleeping beauty of 'Najma' and 'Neelu',
Live pictures of 'Qaiser' and 'Azra'.

Goddess of Beauty on some silver screen,
Standing with green goblet in henna-dyed hands,
As if above in high skies have appeared,
Full moon with splendid colours all around.

This mirror shows me hundred reflections,
Making my dream a reality,
Showing as if high up in the skies have appeared,
A full moon with splendid colours around it.

These mirrors! Call them soothing balm for aching body
and soul,
Or priceless souvenir to be kept for ever.

New Year

New excitement, new year, new life as well,
Let my verve get new awareness too.

Let there be no pain and sorrow of the bygone days,
Let our thoughts be not slave to prejudice and fanaticism.

Let there be an assembly of joy, mirth and dancing
goblets,
O, cup-bearer ! Show generosity to the crowd of tipplers.

Let every orchard bear new blossoming colour,
And every pavement beautiful reflection of stars.

Let lip touch to goblet get intoxicating mirth,
And lovers of youth and beauty eternal ecstacy.

Let the path to progress be opened,
Let courage run surpassing hopes.

Let Earth's hair-parting be star studded,
And chastity of charmful life sparkle.

In every direction, let light of the New Year spread,
And across the whole world, let love and peace pervade.

Kalpana Chawla

It's all new age, it's all new horizon,
It's all new different world.

It's all changed environment,
It's earth that's floating on the sky.

New stars and the new sky,
And it's all new galaxy.

I felt a turbulence in my heart,
And that made me fly up in the sky.

To be an astronaut was my passion,
By the grace of God, I got it fulfilled.

I was filled with a new zeal,
And that took me up on the top.

Anon Death gave me a call:
'You have fulfilled your dream.'

I have a message for all thinking people:
'In death I have my life.'

Know ye? Life is a mystery.
It's only a passion to fly high.

Gift - 1

What gift should I give you, my darling
On this Republic Day?

The coronation of Tilak,
Fragrant flowers of Bapu's tenets,
Dazzle of Moti's Jawahar,
Everything worth salutation.
What gift should I give you, my darling
On this Republic Day?

Remember the brave Bhagat Singh,
Every moment Shekhar be 'azad'
Ashfaq be cheerful,
World of Bismil be prosperous,
O! my dear, my country is a beautiful flower.
What gift should I give you, my darling
On this Republic Day?

Together we have decorated our country,
Together we have made it priceless,
It's always close to our hearts,
Such is our darling - India.

Gift - 2

Every gift priceless
On this Republic Day, my darling.

A dream of golden India,
A symbol of paradise on earth,
Each moment of joy and delight,
A world of happiness, my darling.

Each evening a new one - star-studded,
Weather enchanting, my darling.
Every gift priceless,
On this Republic Day, my darling.

I know you sent me gifts,
Of all hue and colour.
You gifted me Tagore's poetry,
Bankim's Taraana,
And many more,
Yes, you sent me countless gifts.
But alas! some snatcher
Ran away with all these.
Every gift priceless
On this Republic Day, my darling.

Grave Moments

He'll ask about the rising and sinking moments,
Ask why the blooming life faded,
Who burnt it? Who destroyed it?
Know not what questions he may ask.

Where were the beautiful couple deboarded?
What! who looted the golden chain and the silver-studded stars?
Who else besides the driver killed?
He'll ask about the beloved ones,
Know not what questions he may ask.

That big blast and the train loot,
Life taken out from some in that gory loot and the stampede,
Hotly debated in the Assembly,
Those 'care-takers' showing concern about the nation,
Know not what questions he may ask.

The terrific quake rocking Japan,
Thousands died, tears relentlessly rolling down,
Each heart torn, laden with grief,
And then those hearts stopped throbbing; why? what
happened?
Know not what questions he may ask.

If Life exists, so does Death,
The boat is bound to sink in deep.

Rainy Season

Looks my darling wet and drenched,
Its mood romantic like a rainbow,
The wandering cloud a preface to nimbus.
Rising waves up against the river bank,
Maybe the captives overcome the captors.
Watch the droplets oozing down banyan branches.

Shivering moon wrapped in a cloudy duvet,
Nestless birds drooping on a jackfruit tree,
Night's hairy locks gleaming from the sky- top,
Splendid rows of lamps and countless candles,
Everywhere that flickering gleam of glow-worms,
Seems it's a festival of lights in a dark deep jungle.

Chirping of cricket - a precursor to the poetic presentation,
A soft smile on the ploughman's lips,
Boundless hopes from the thriving life,
Oh, this mirth and the madness, all from you dear!

The Earthly Heaven

Moon: pale faced
Stars: dim
Desert, mountain: dusky
Garden: treeless
River: parched
Day: gloomy
Night: sinister
Tree: beheaded
Branch: fruitless
Plants, creepers: colourless
Birds: clipped winged
Beasts: famished
Musical instruments: silent
Assembly: defenceless
Earthly heaven: on the edge of hell
Man: helpless

Yashodhara

Where is the prime of garden's existence when Gautam
has short life?
I saw the stigma of autumn on the flower's ornate face,
I saw strange shade of firmament and strange did I see the
condition of the world,
Delusion is continuous and follows the course of life.

Flame of luxurious life burning in the feasting party,
But the search of Truth laid the trap of darkness.
You chose separation but I craved for bonds,
Spending my days in Rahul's care.

Why did you desert me after accepting as life partner?
You were to adhere to the faithfulness of promise,
You were to hold my hands in support,
If you were to see God, why you turned your face from
the world?

Forsaking God's creation to get His love,
Look! some have parched lips but you have your fill.

Eerie Silence

Friends! She too was a splendid musical instrument,
Her songs adorned the party,
The clinking of her anklets comforted the courtiers,
She was the voice of the diva.

Under her dark black locks,
Know not how many nobles and robbers got comfort,
Know not how many lechers got solace,
Know not how many pleasure-seekers got eternal happiness.

Though ignorant of the eventual ending,
She continued dancing and singing.
Life continued smiling the whole night,
Unaware of the morning trap.

Behold, what an eerie silence at the crossroad today!
Alas! the broken harp suddenly gone silent.

Longing

Every patch of parched land longing for rain,
Newly wed bride longing for her groom,
Forests, mountains, meadows, dried up waterfalls,
Every patch of parched land longing for rain.
Spring riding on the shoulders of autumn,
Hope in the womb of dismay,
Every patch of parched land longing for rain,
Newly wed bride longing for her groom.

Queen of Beauty

Queen of beauty - a fancy, a dream
A flower, fragrance, moonlight, an endearing kiss
Jasmine, daisy, lily or rose,
Queen of beauty - a fancy, a dream.
Red rose wine, a full moon encased
Rhythmic dance, melodious song, bar girls of today,
Queen of beauty - a fancy, a dream,
A flower, fragrance, moonlight, an endearing kiss.

Camps of the Aged

Lots of bright light left in otherwise flickering lamps
Goblets of heart still brimming but with etiquette,
Lots of attraction still in the folds of old,
Lots of bright light left in otherwise flickering lamps
Lots of joy, mirth, tranquility and peace,
Bound by one thread of age - their own and the unknown.
Lots of bright light left in otherwise flickering lamps,
Goblets of heart still brimming but with etiquette.

Life's Footpath

Steps marching forward on life's narrow path,
Seems every field a sight of pain and anguish,
Time a thorn, life a sorrow,
Steps marching forward on life's narrow path.
Only occasionally, calmness descends
In otherwise scattered sand of mortal remains all over,
Steps marching forward on life's narrow path,
Seems every field a sight of pain and anguish

Marching Steps of a Village

Marching steps of the village vying cities,
Though deep in pensive thoughts are its narrow footpaths,
And the silent old banyan tree with moist eyes;
Still are the marching steps of the village vying cities.
Men, women, old and young - all filled with grief'
And no one to listen to the wailing of birds,
Still are the marching steps of the village vying cities,
Though deep in pensive thoughts are its narrow footpaths.